Gerhard Lang

Airbus
Aircraft Since 1972

Airbus

Aircraft Since 1972

Gerhard Lang

Pen & Sword
AVIATION

First published in Great Britain in 2015 by
Pen & Sword Aviation
an imprint of
Pen & Sword Books Ltd
47 Church Street
Barnsley
South Yorkshire
S70 2AS

ISBN 978 1 78383 171 5

A CIP catalogue record for this book is available from the British Library

Typeset in Ehrhardt by
Mac Style Ltd, Bridlington, East Yorkshire
Printed and bound in Malta by Gutenberg Press

Pen & Sword Books Ltd incorporates the imprints of Pen & Sword
Archaeology, Atlas, Aviation, Battleground, Discovery, Family History, History,
Maritime, Military, Naval, Politics, Railways, Select, Transport, True Crime,
and Fiction, Frontline Books, Leo Cooper, Praetorian Press, Seaforth
Publishing and Wharncliffe.

For a complete list of Pen & Sword titles please contact
PEN & SWORD BOOKS LIMITED
47 Church Street, Barnsley, South Yorkshire, S70 2AS, England
E-mail: enquiries@pen-and-sword.co.uk
Website: www.pen-and-sword.co.uk

Photo credits: Photos were provided by the following firms/persons: Airbus
Industrie; Airbus Industrie/H.Goussé; Air France/Philippe Delafosse;
EADS/CASA; Germanwings; Hamburg International; LAGL-Dokumentation;
Gerhard Lang; Lufthansa; Lufthansa/Gerd Rebenich; Christoph Wolff;
A.Doumjou/Exm Company

Contents

Introduction 6

Airbus A300 12

SATIC A300B4-608ST Beluga 20

Airbus A310 26

Airbus A318 36

Airbus A319 44

Airbus A320 52

Airbus A321 60

Airbus A330-200/-300 68

Airbus A340-200/-300 76

Airbus A340-500/-600 84

Airbus A350 92

Airbus A380 104

Airbus Military A400M 118

Airbus Industrie, an offspring enterprise of EADS (European Aeronautic Defence and Space Company) came into being on 18 December 1970 by way of a merger between Aerospatiale and the Deutsche Airbus GmbH. The head office is in Toulouse. The various centres of production are to be found in Germany, France, Great Britain and Spain. About 57,000 persons are employed by Airbus at the present time.

The French Aerospatiale resulted from the fusion of Sud Aviation and Nord Aviation.

Already in Germany in 1965 the working pool Arbeitsgemeinschaft Airbus had been set up from the firms Siebel, Bölkow, Dornier, Flugzeug-Union Süd, Hamburger Flugzeugbau (HFB), Messerschmitt and Vereinigte Flugtechnische Werke (VFW). Around the same time Messerschmitt, Bölkow and the Hamburger Flugzeugbau had merged as Messerschmitt-Bölkow-Blohm GmbH (MBB), while the Vereinigte Flugtechnische Werke and Fokker merged as VFW-Fokker. The Arbeitsgemeinschaft Airbus became the

The A300 prototype, the F-WUAB, during its maiden flight on 28 October 1972.

A310-300 in works livery- F-WWCA went later to Air Niugini.

Deutsche Airbus GmbH, owned jointly by MBB (60%), Dornier (20%) and VFW-Fokker (20%).

The first talks on the mutual development of a passenger aircraft were held between Aerospatiale, Deutsche Airbus GmbH and the British company Hawker-Siddeley in 1965. Airbus Industrie was founded on 18 December 1970 by Aerospatiale in partnership with Deutsche Airbus GmbH. Hawker-Siddeley was not directly involved but developed and delivered large wing sections.

A320 during testing.

Formation flight of an A319, A320 and A321, the latter being the prototype F-WWIA.

A318 prototype with registration marking F-WWIA. This machine was equipped with CFM-56-5 engines.

The A319 prototype F-WWDB flew for the first time on 25 August 1995.

In 1971 the Spanish CASA and in 1979 British Aerospace joined the consortium. On 19 May 1989 Dornier, MTU (Motor-and-Turbine Union) and parts of AEG merged to become Deutsche Aerospace AG (DASA). This entity was renamed Daimler-Benz Aerospace AG after the takeover by Daimler-Benz on 1 January 1995. The shares in Airbus Industrie were now split as follows: Aerospatiale 37.9%, DASA 37.9%, British Aerospace 20% and CASA 4.2%. In the year 2000, DASA, Aerospatiale and CASA joined EADS with headquarters in the Netherlands.

In the mid-1990s a weak dollar led to substantial upheavals at Airbus. Under the reorganization programme "Dolores" (Dollar Low Rescue), a large number of jobs were lost, especially in Germany.

In 2001 Airbus transformed itself into an independent company subject to French Law with head offices at Toulouse-Blagnac. 80% of the shares were held by EADS and 20% by BAE Systems. In 2001 for the first time Airbus had more orders for aircraft than Boeing and thus became the world market leader in passenger

An A330-300 in flight.

aircraft. On 9 September 2005 Airbus delivered the four-thousandth aircraft, an A330-300 for Deutsche Lufthansa.

In 2005 completing the A320 at Tiajin in China was considered for the first time.

There was another crisis in 2006 when fuselage sections for the A380 were delivered to Toulouse from Finkenwerder with short-length cabling, which led to substantial delays with the A380.

In 2006 BAE Systems sold its holdings in Airbus Industrie to EADS. Since and September 2006 EADS has been the sole shareholder in Airbus.

In the framework of the programme of economies known as "Power 8", to make good the losses caused by the problems with the A380 completion, in January 2007 it was announced that various factories were to be sold and the workforce reduced by 8,000 to 15,000 employees. Amongst the factories to be sold were four in Germany at Augsburg, Laupheim, Nordenham and Varel.

Airbus Industrie was and is producing the following aircraft types in various versions: A300, A310, A318, A319, A320, A321, A330, A340, A350, A380 and A400M.

A300/A310 was turned out at Toulouse. By the end of production in 2007 a total of 561 A300's and 251 A310's had been delivered. Both at

F-WWAI was the first A340-300.

The A340-600 is the world's longest passenger aircraft.

Toulouse and Hamburg-Finkenwerder there are final assembly lines for the A320 family, to which the A318, A319, A320 and A321 belong.

Up to 31 January 2009 there were orders for 83 A318 aircraft (67 delivered), and for the A319 1527 units (1142 delivered). The A320 is the best seller to date – 3952 ordered (2051 delivered). 751 A321 are on order (494 delivered). The A330 and A340 are being produced again at Toulouse.

There are orders for 1012 A330's (590 delivered) and 385 A340's (361 delivered). The A380 is being manufactured at Toulouse at Hamburg-Finkenwerder, 202 are on order at the present time (21 delivered).

The final assembly line for the A400M is at Seville in Spain. Total sales by Airbus Industrie of all models is 9209 aircraft (5534 delivered).

Imposing photo of an A380 during an air display before the Aerosalon at Paris-Le Bourget.

Computer graphic of an A400M as a paratroop carrier on active military service.

A380

Airbus A300

The A300B was developed as a middle distance passenger aircraft. It was the first of its class to be designed for two through-passages in the fuselage and to carry unit-containers in the lower deck. The first prototype, A300B1 made its maiden flight on 28 October 1972, the second prototype on 5 February 1973.

During the 16-month testing phase, decentralized production was set up. Aérospatiale built the cockpit, the nose, section of the central fuselage and the engine pylons. Large sections of the fuselage were completed at MBB and the final assembly of the fuselage was done at Hamburg-Finkenwerder. The fitting of the wings, linked systems and moving parts was handled at Bremen. British Aerospace designed and built the wings. The elevators and smaller construction groups were manufactured by CASA. All prefabricated parts were brought to Toulouse for final assembly and subsequent

Air Inter was amongst the first operators of the A300. This machine is photographed approaching Paris-Charles de Gaulle.

D-AIAA was the first A300B2 to be delivered to Lufthansa.

An Airbus A300B4 in the Iberia livery.

flight testing. Large sections were airlifted by four "Super Guppy" transporters.

A300 was completed in two basic versions: the A300B2 for a maximum range of 3700 kms, and the A300B4 for a maximum range of 5300 kms with an additional fuel tank in the fuselage. When the first A300B2-100's were delivered in 1974, these had an all-up weight of 137 tonnes. Improvements such as additional Krüger flaps along the wing nose and better braking systems enabled this weight to be increased to 142 tonnes.

On the A300B4 as well, the all-up weight was increased from 150 tonnes to 165 tonnes by strengthening the mainframe and equipping it with more powerful engines. The A300B4-100 was fitted with three-section leading edge slats, leading edge (Krüger) flaps, three-section

Continental was one of the early North American Airbus clients.

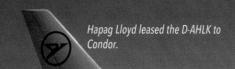

Hapag Lloyd leased the D-AHLK to Condor.

Hapag Lloyd's D-AHLJ on the apron at Hannover in April 1988.

landing flaps and braking flaps. The A300B4-200 had a reinforced structure and was delivered from May 1976.

52 aircraft of the A300B2 were built and 185 A300B4's. Another three A300C4 Convertibles and two A300C4/F freighters were sold. Both versions have a freight door 3.58 metres wide

Only the logo on the rudder shows that this is an A300B4 of Egypt Air.

Monarch, one of the major British charter companies, also chose the A300-600R.

on the left side of the fuselage forward and can take about 42 tonnes of freight.

In December 1980 Airbus Industrie announced the A300-600. This would replace the A300B2 and A300B4 forerunners from 1984.

The A300-600 benefited from all the experience and improvements realized in the A310. New, more efficient engine plant, changes to the wing profile and savings in weight by the greater use of artificial materials

15 ■

An A300-600 of Olympic Airlines at Stuttgart rolling for take-off.

led to such an increase in efficiency overall that the aircraft could now be used for long-range flights.

As compared to the A300B the fuselage behind the wings was lengthened by 1.59 metres and offered seats for 257 passengers. A new, shorter tail cone resulted in an overall increase of fuselage length of only 0.53 metres. The elevators and trimming tanks were replicated completely from the A310-300.

The fully-electronic two-man cockpit with its display screens is almost identical to that of the A310. The new auxiliary turbine (APU), simple Fowler flaps and the triangular "wingtip-fences" also come from the A310. The A300-600 also received a new braking control system.

The lower deck can take either 23 LD-3 containers each with a load of 1-tonne, or ten LD-3's and four pallets with a total load weight of 30 tonnes.

The A300-600 made its maiden flight on 8 July 1983. In April 1984, Saudia was the first

American Airlines bought 34 A300-600R's.

airline to receive the A300-600. The A300-600R with a range of 7500 kms was the second version to arrive on the market. This aircraft has the prescribed special permission for extensive flights over the sea (ETOPS).

The first client and also the major operator of the A300-600R was American Airlines with a fleet of 35 aircraft. The first machine entered commercial service in May 1988. In June 1988 Japan Air System took over its eighteenth A300-600R, and also has another nine A300B2's and

aircraft. The freighter version has a reinforced cabin floor, a 9g crash-net, a freight-room smoke alarm installation and on the left side of the fuselage forward an extra freight door of 2.57 x 3.58 metres dimension. The fuselage has no cabin windows nor door except for the

An A300-600R of Tunisair shortly after leaving the ground at Stuttgart.

eight A300B4's. The operational reliability of these aircraft was 99.8%.

In 1991 Federal Express ordered fifteen A300-600F's, later increased to thirty-six, built as pure freighters, in contrast to the passenger

forward two. The maximum useful weight is 54,780 kgs for a range of 3520 kms.

The A300-600 engine plant is two CF6-80C2 turbines regulated by a computer digital system. Maiden flight was on 2 December

17 ■

The A300-600 model replaced production of the A300B2/B4. This is a machine of IranAir.

Three Thai airlines A300-600R aircraft can be seen in this photo.

The A300-600R has a range of 7,500 kms.

Airbus A300-600R	
Manufacturer:	Airbus Industrie, France.
Purpose:	Middle and Long-distance passenger aircraft for from 259 to 361 passengers.
Crew:	Two pilots and eight to ten flight attendants.
Engine plant:	2 x General Electric CF6-80C2A1, each with 262.4 kN (26,762 kp): or Pratt & Whitney PW 4156 each with 249 kN (25,401 kp) standing thrust with reverse thrust installation.
Wingspan:	44.84 m.
Length:	54.08 m.
Height:	16.62 m.
Wing area:	260 sq.m.
Wing loading:	660.4 kgs/sq.m.
Weight empty:	89.5 tonnes.
Maximum take-off weight:	171.7 tonnes.
Maximum landing weight:	140 tonnes.
Maximum payload:	44 tonnes 178 kgs.
Tank capacity:	73,000 litres.
Maximum cruising speed:	890 kms/hr at 7620 m.
Economic cruising speed:	860 kms/hr.
Landing speed:	255 kms/hr
Service Ceiling:	12,200 m.
Rate of climb:	600 m/min
Take-off run:	2700 m
Landing path:	2000 m.
Range:	5000 kms fully loaded: 7600 kms with full tanks and 225 passengers.
Fuel consumption:	8250 litres/hr.

1993, the first machine being delivered on 27 April 1994. In September 1998 Airbus Industrie received from United Parcel Service (UPS) a further major order for thirty A300-600F's and thirty options.

A fine photo of the third A300-608ST in flight.

Four A300-608ST's were built to airlift large structural parts.

Satic A300B4-608ST Beluga (white-whale)

The Airbus subsidiary Special Aircraft Transport International Company (SATIC) built at Colomier/Toulouse the A300-608ST Beluga (ST=Super Transporter) to airlift large structural parts such as cockpits, fuselage rear parts, wings, rudders and elevators. SATIC was set up on 20 October 1991. DASA and Aérospatiale were involved in equal shares in the new project. The contract between Airbus Industrie and SATIC for the development and building of the aircraft was signed on 7 February 1992. SATIC accepted responsibility for design, development, production and delivery.

The aircraft are used for transport flights between the Airbus locations. The A300-608ST replaces the Aero Spacelines Super Guppy, a conversion from the Boeing KC-97, in service since 1972. The A300-600R was the basis for the new aircraft, the lower half of the fuselage, wings, undercarriage and pressure cabin being copied from it. The fuselage upper part from the cabin floor upwards was newly designed for a loading volume requirement of around 1400 cubic metres. The newly designed fuselage upper-shell was delivered by CASA and the Elbe aircraft works. The cockpit was relocated to the lower floor surface to create room for the approximately 100 sq.metres area of loading hatch. When the freight door is open to its maximum 67°, the nose section has a height of 16.78 metres. Thus unwieldy large items can be loaded and unloaded without causing a major problem. The freight box has a diameter of 7.4

metres and is 37.7 metres long, its floor 5.43 metres wide. Payload is 47 tonnes. The freight box can accommodate for example a completed pair of A340 wings weighing 42 tonnes.

The elevator gear was reinforced and fitted with additional tailwing-end discs to improve the effectiveness of the original and enhance flight stability. The rudder was also set higher up.

A better performing version of the basic engine plant, the General Electric CF6-80C2 with 26,765 kp thrust is installed. Fully laden

the A300-608ST has a range of 1700 kms at 750 kms/hr. The range is increased to 4600 kms with half payload.

Work on building the first A300-608ST began in September 1992. The machine was displayed to the public for the first time on 23 June 1994 and took off at 0902 hrs on 13 September 1994 for its maiden flight. This flight lasted four hours 21 minutes. On board were Chief Test Pilot Gilbert Defer, Lucien Benard as co-pilot and test engineers Jean-Pierre Flamant and Didier Ronceray.

154 test flights were made totalling 335 hours and were completed by the September 1995 deadline. The A300B4-608ST's are intended for 70,000 flight hours corresponding to 36,000 flights.

The second machine made its maiden flight on 26 March 1996 and the third flight on 21 April 1997. The final assembly of the fourth machine began in February 1998. As compared to the Super Guppy, the freight

Airbus A300-608ST Beluga	
Manufacturer:	Special Aircraft Transport International Company (SATIC), Colomier/Toulouse, France.
Purpose:	Freight aircraft.
Crew:	Two pilots.
Engine plant:	2 x GEC CF6-80C2A8 turbofans each with 262.4 kN.
Wingspan:	44.84 m.
Wing area:	260 sq.m.
Height:	17.24 m.
Length:	56.16 m.
Payload:	45.5 tonnes.
Length freight box:	37.7 m.
Diameter freight box:	7.4 m.
Volume freight box:	1400 cubic m.
Maximum take-off weight:	155 tonnes.
Cruising speed:	780 kms/hr
Range:	1666 kms.
Take-off run:	1950 m
Weight empty:	86.5 tonnes.

handling times are reduced by about 180 minutes to 45 minutes. On 24 November 1996 an A300-608ST on a commercial trip carried a 40-tonne section of the international space station.

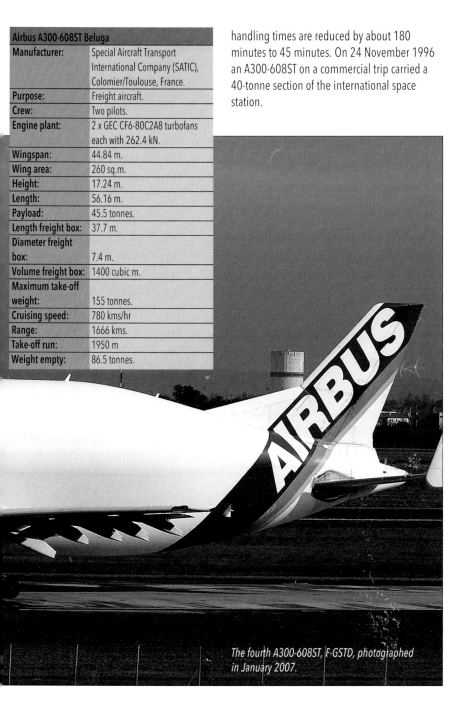

The fourth A300-608ST, F-GSTD, photographed in January 2007.

The Turkish airline THY had seven A310-200 in its fleet.

Airbus A310

At the instigation of several airlines in July 1978 Airbus Industrie began with the development of the A310, a smaller version of the A300 for short hauls. Lufthansa and Swissair were the launching customers of the project.

The A310 was the first step towards an Airbus family. The fuselage cross-section diameter of 5.64 metres of the A310 corresponds to that of the A300 but is shorter by 13 cross-frames (corresponding to 7 metres) and offers seating for 178 to 280 passengers. The fuselage has only two passenger doors either side. The new wings and smaller wingspan were developed

by British Aerospace and fitted with new engine mounts. The outer ailerons on the wings disappeared. As compared to the A300 the new wings enabled a saving of 20% in fuel consumption. The use of carbon fibre compound for parts brought a saving in weight of about 500 kgs. Other differences were modifications to the wheel-chassis, the rear and a smaller tail unit. The freight box in the space under the floor of the A310 has a volume of 60 sq.metres. It can accommodate fourteen LD-3 containers or three pallets and seven containers. The A310-200 fuel tanks hold a maximum of 55,000 litres, those of the A310-300 up to 61,100 litres, or up to 68,100 litres with a supplementary tank. For engine plant

An A310 of Aerolineas Argentinas landing.

there is a choice between the Pratt & Whitney PW JT9D-7R4D1 or PW4152 and the General Electric GE CF6-80C2A2.

The A310 corresponds to the state of technology of the 1980s and was the first wide-ranging commercial aircraft to have a digitalized two-man cockpit. A large part of the instrumentation was given over to multi-function displays. The A310 has an electronic flight instrument system (EFIS) and a flight management system (FMS).

Because of the similarity between the A310 and A300 in many areas no prototype was built.

Both aircraft types, the A300-600 and the A310, were manufactured on the same assembly line. There are four versions of the A310: the A310-200 is the basic version; the A310.200C (Convertible) is a mixed passenger/freight version with a freight door in the forward cabin area. The aircraft can be converted into a full freighter with a 40-tonne payload within 15 hours. The A-310-200F is a freighter and the A310-300 a passenger version with extended range, increased take-off weight, a trimming tank in the stabilizer and optional additional tanks for extreme distances.

An A310-300 of the Canadian Air Transat after just landing at Frankfurt.

SATA International uses its A310-300's amongst other routes on flights between Stuttgart and the Azores.

The first A310 with the registration F-WZLH was rolled out and flown for the first time on 16 February 1982 at Toulouse, and was delivered to Swissair as HB-IPE on 21 March 1984. The second machine F-WZLI flew on 13 May 1982 and went to Air France in 1986. The third A310 with test marking F-WZLJ went to Lufthansa as D-AICA on 9 March 1984.

By then Swissair (HB-IPA on 25 March 1983) and Lufthansa (D-AICB on 29 June 1983) already had their first A310's with which they founded the commercial line. Lufthansa chose the GEC CF6-80 turbine, Swissair the Pratt & Whitney JT9D-74R. These engines have a high bypass ratio, a negligible difference in fuel consumption, a good thrust/weight ratio and in operation are environmentally friendly and quiet. The Rolls-Royce RB.211-524B4 is also available if desired.

The A310-200 delivered to Sabena on 1 March 1984 had an increased take-off weight of 142 tonnes. This machine had a range of

A Cyprus Airways A310-300 landing at Zürich.

The A310-324 (ET) pictured here has been with the Delta fleet since 1993.

6500 kms. Martinair accepted the first A310-200C in December 1984.

After 85 units had been delivered, the production of the A310-200 was terminated. The A310-300 succeeded it with an increased take-off weight of 157 tonnes and operates on intercontinental routes. It differs from earlier versions by an additional 6100-litre fuel tank in the stabilizer, a tail fin of carbon fibre (CFK), winglets to reduce air resistance and a revised cockpit layout.

The trim tank in the tail unit not only serves to increase the amount of fuel but also for the optimal trim in flight. An increase in range is possible by installing an additional tank in the rear cargo hold to provide a total of 68,100 litres.

The Spanish tour company Air Plus also operates the A310-300.

The first A310-300 completed its maiden flight on 8 July 1985. It was Swissair again, in February 1986, which was first to accept this version into passenger service. Austrian Airlines took two A310-300's on 16 July 1989 for the service between Vienna and New York, and Tokyo. The first use on passenger airlines by Western commercial aircraft in the then Eastern

The Czechoslovak Airline took over its first A310-300 in February 1991.

Bloc was begun by Interflug and CSA from the summer of 1989, each with three A310-300's. The A310 was the first Western airliner to receive licensing from the Russians, in October 1991. Up to the present, eleven A310 have been delivered to Aeroflot, three to Uzbekistan Airlines, one to Armenian Airlines, one to Kyrgistan Airlines and two to Sakha Airlines.

Flugbereitschaft BMVg has seven A310's. Three of these aircraft are the former A310's of

Interflug converted by Lufthansa Technik into VIP-transporters. Their sphere of operations includes the transport of persons and materials and humanitarian projects. From mid-1998 the aircraft were converted to the Multi-Role Transporter (MRT) Standard by EADS at Dresden and Lufthansa Technik at Hamburg, involving the building of a large freight hatch in the upper deck and ball-bearing mats on the freight hold floor for swifter loading and to facilitate conversion for various purposes. In a very short time the VUK model (Transport for the Wounded and Sick) can be prepared for MEDEC (Medical Evacuation) operations. The first MRT A310-304 was the 10+24 "Otto Lilienthal" available from the end of March 1999. It was used the following month in emergency flights for Kosovo refugees. Further such flights made were the return of the seriously hurt victims of the bomb explosion on the Tunisian island of Djerba and the evacuation of intensive-care patients from the hospitals in Dresden threatened by the Elbe floods during the catastrophe in eastern Germany in August 1992.

Airbus A310-300		Sweep:	28°
Manufacturer:	Airbus Industrie, Blagnac, France.	Wing loading:	713.6 kgs/sq.m
Purpose:	Short, middle and long haul passenger aircraft for 178 to 280 passengers, two pilots and up to ten flight attendants.	Weight empty:	81.2 tonnes.
		Max. take-off weight:	150 tonnes.
		Max. landing weight:	123 tonnes.
		Maximum payload:	34 tonnes.
Engine plant:	2 x GEC CF6-80A3, each rated 238.0 kN (24267 kp), or CF6-80C2A4 each rated 262.4 kN (26762 kp) or 2 x Pratt & Whitney PW4152 each rated at 231.2 kN (23586 kp) or PW4165A each rated at 249.1 kn (25400 kp) standing thrust with reverse thrust installation.	Tank capacity:	68,100 litres.
		Max. cruising speed:	897 kms/hr at 10,670 m.
		Economic cruising speed:	850 kms/hr at 11,280 m.
		Landing speed:	260 kms/hr
		Service ceiling:	12,550 m.
		Rate of climb:	780 m/min.
		Take-off run:	3 kms.
		Landing path:	1900 m.
Wingspan:	43.9 m	Range:	8000 kms with full payload; 9,100 kms with full tanks and 172 passengers.
Length:	46.66 m		
Height:	15.81 m		
Fuselage diameter:	5.64 m.	Fuel consumption:	5,200 litres/hr.
Wing area:	219.0 sq.m		

Aeroflot received its first A310 at the beginning of the 1990s.

Airbus A318

In September 1998 at the Farnborough Air Show, Airbus Industrie announced the beginning of development work on the twin-jet A318. This is a shortened version of the A319. Thus it was first known as A319M5, M5 meaning "minus five cross-frames". It was intended basically as a competitor to the Boeing 717. Airline companies which already use Airbus aircraft can offer their clients the same comfort and standard of technology on a inland and regional routes.

The first orders came from Air France, which on 26 April 1999 signed a contract to buy fifteen with the option for ten more. The CFM56-5B was chosen for the engine plant. Ai

Air France uses A318-100's for its short haul flights.

France accepted delivery of its first A318, F-GUGA, on 9 October 2003.

The cockpit corresponds to that of other aircraft of the A320 and A330/340 breed so that the pilots need little or no conversion training. LCD (Liquid Crystal Display) screens replaced CRT (Cathode Ray Tube) screens. The A318 also has Fly-by-Wire controls.

Compared to the A319, the fuselage forward of the wings was shortened by 0.79 metres, and behind the wings by 1.59 metres so that fuselage length is now 31.44 metres. This meant that the freight door had to be smaller with a width of 1.22 metres.

Retaining the fuselage structure of the A320-family does bring some disadvantages in its train. This structure for the A321 means a more robust form and 24 tonnes more weight than

The A318 destined for LAN Chile is equipped with PW6122 engines.

with the A318. In its turn the A318 is considerably heavier than is really necessary, a fact which makes itself apparent in its fuel consumption and higher landing charges. In order to protect against yaw the rudder gear had to be enlarged by 0.5 metres in breadth and 0.8 metres in height. The A318 cabin has a two-class system, 107 passengers being accommodated eight in First Class and 99 Economy Class. In a single-class arrangement 117 passengers could be carried or 117 Economy Class for charter-flight companies. The A318 is offered in six variations. With this spread of variants Airbus is appealing especially to the North American

The A318 prototype fitted with CFM56-5 turbines rolling out to start its second maiden flight at Finkenwerder.

commerical lines which like operational flexibility with a choice of payload. As according to the wishes of the customer, the engine plant can be the newly-developed PW6000 turbine or the reduced performance CFM56-5B. On 4 August 1999 a contract was signed with CFM for the equipping of aircraft with this engine.

Completion of the first components began at the end of October and on 21 May 2001 fuselage sections 13 and 14 were delivered to Saint-Nazaire. The final assembly of the prototype began on 9 August 2001 at Finkenwerder. The two PW6000 engines were installed in October 2001. The first prototype fitted with these turbines, registration F-WWIA, made its maiden flight at Hamburg-Finkenwerder on 15 January 2002. Time spent in the air was 3 hours 44 minutes. The machine was flown by Finkenwerder Airbus Works Chief Pilot Bernd Schaefer, acting as Captain, and Airbus Chief Pilot Jacques Rosay as co-pilot. Flight engineers Manfred Birnfeld, Hermann Schmöckel and Bernhard Kamps were also aboard.

On this first flight the entire programme, the range of speeds from the minimum speed to the highest permitted of Mach 0.82 was tested together with the flight control system, the flaps and undercarriage. The service ceiling of 11,890 metres was reached. Around seven tonnes of flight testing instruments were carried aboard the 57.5-tonne aircraft, fitted with 94 kilometres of cabling. Further tests were carried out at Toulouse. The second prototype had PW6124 turbines for its maiden flight on 7 June 2002.

The length of flight testing for the first prototype was scheduled for 450 hours, 300 hours for the second aircraft. The acceptance period for the CFM56 engines with which the other members of the A320 family were to be fitted was expected to be 150 flight hours.

Because of problems with the Pratt & Whitney PW6000 turbines the test programme had to be changed. The new turbine consumed much more fuel than the manufacturer had predicted. This was due to the effective level of the high pressure compressor being too low. The first prototype had its maiden flight with the PW6000 but was refitted with the CFM56-5B in June 2002 and resumed the certification programme on 29 August 2002. After all problems had been resolved, the first prototype switched back to the PW6000 in the autumn of 2004 and flew with the modified turbines on 9 December 2004.

On 23 May 2003 the A318 flown with CFM56-5B turbines was licensed by the European JAA. The US FAA licence followed in June. The first A318 was delivered to Frontier Airlines on 22 July 2003.

The aircraft was the 2000th machine of the A320 family to be delivered. Because of the terror attacks of 11 September 2001 in New York many airlines reviewed their planning and some cut back drastically their orders to Airbus. After British Airways changed its order for twelve A318's to the same number of A321's, and Egyptair now wanted five A320's instead of A318's, the number of A318's on order was sharply reduced. As another version the A318 "Elite" was offered in 2005 as a business jet with fourteen or eighteen seats.

Frontier Airlines decorates the rudder of its aircraft with animal motifs.

A318		Maximum payload:	13,340 kgs.
Manufacturer:	Airbus Industrie, France, Germany, Britain, Spain.	Maximum weight less fuel:	54.5 tonnes.
Purpose:	Short-haul commercial aircraft for 99 to 129 passengers.	Maximum rolling weight:	59.4 tonnes.
Crew:	Two pilots.	Maximum tank capacity:	23,860 litres.
Engine plant:	2 x Pratt & Whitney PW6122/PW6124 or CFM International CFM56-5B/P each with 89 kN to 102.3 kN (9070 to 10430 kP) thrust.	Cruising speed:	840 kms/hr.
		Service ceiling:	13,650 m.
		Take-off run:	1350-1400 m.
		Landing run:	1340 m.
Spannweite:	34.10 m.	Range:	2800 kms with maximum payload.
Length:	31.45 m.		
Height:	12.55 m.		
Wing area:	122.40 sq.m.		
Fuselage diameter:	3.96 m.		
Cabin dimensions:	21.38 m x 3.7 m.		
Weight empty:	39035 kgs.		
Maximum take-off weight:	61.5 tonnes.		
Maximum landing weight:	57.5 tonnes.		

The A318 Elite business jet.

Iberia uses the A319-100 on its local European flights.

Airbus A319

The A319 belongs to the Airbus family of standard-fuselage aircraft made up of the A318, A319, A320 and A321. This makes it possible for the airlines to match passenger capacity to the traffic. The A319 is used primarily on short and medium haul routes.

All four aircraft types have the same basic cockpit and flight characteristics. Normally the pilots' qualification covers them for all these aircraft so that no additional training is required when they change machines.

Equally the ground staff can handle all types leading to substantial savings in costs at the airlines. CFM International CFM56-5B6 or International Aero Engines V2500-A5 turbines are fitted which in the case of the A319 are throttled to 104.5 kN each. This reduction in power became necessary to match the flight attitude of the lighter machine to that of the two larger types.

The first A319-100 delivered to Lufthansa was given the name "Frankfurt/Oder".

The A319 is based on the A320. All modifications to the A320 and A321 were taken into account and the type is therefore very modern. In principle this is a series of aircraft of similar design but with varying fuselage lengths and weights manufactured on the module system. The proportion of parts common to all models is around 95%.

As compared to the A320, the fuselage of the A319 has been shortened by removing individual segments ahead of and behind the wing totalling 3.73 metres. The difference between the A319 and the A321 is 10.67 metres. The elevators, ailerons and rudder are complete replicas of the A320. Even the wings with their integral tanks were used, and so the A319 has the same fuel tank volume as the A320. As already mentioned the cockpits are also to a great extent identical. An important new installation is the Global Positioning System (GPS). The satellite navigational system has replaced the inertial system as the principal

US Airways bought a total of 109 A319-100's.

navigational aid. An additional installation is a larger data bank for navigation. The flight control computer of the Fly-by-Wire system was suitable for the aircraft and the Flight Management and Guidance Computer received the new software.

In the typical two-class arrangment with a single central aisle the A319 has seating for 124 passengers. The passenger cabin has two installations for regulating temperature and additional heating in the region of the forward door. In the underfloor freight hold there is space for four LD3-46 containers. The internal fittings and final assembly of the A319 are handled by EADS at Hamburg together with the A321.

The start of the A319 programme was announced officially on 10 June 1993. The final assembly of the first A319 was begun on 23 March 1995. The aircraft was rolled out on 24

The Germanwings fleet is made up mostly of A319-100's.

August and took off on its maiden flight of three hours 50 minutes at Hamburg a day later. Pilot was Chief Test Pilot Udo Günzel, co-pilot Claude Lelaie and flight engineers aboard were Fernando Alonso, Manfred Brinfeld and Gerard Desbois. For flight testing they transferred to Toulouse on 29 August. The second aircraft began testing on 31 October 1995 and lasted around 650 flying hours. On the return flight from a demonstration tour to South America, the A319 flew nonstop for 6590 kilometres. On 10 April 1996 the JAA licensed the A319 with CFM56-5B turbines. Only thirty months' development had been needed from the start of the programme to the first commercial flight with Swissair in April 1996. On 14 January 1997 Air Canada received the second of 35 A319's on order. On the delivery flight the aircraft covered 6645 kilometres to Winnipeg in nine hours five minutes, a new world record. On 14 February the 120-minutes ETOPS licence for the A319 with CFM56-5 and also V2500-A5 turbines was received. An A319, the 1500th Airbus Industrie aircraft, was received by

An A319-100 in the Eurowings livery.

Lufthansa on 18 February 1997. The 100th A319, works number 871, came off the Hamburg production line in August 1998 and was delivered to United Airlines.

The Swiss company PrivatAir runs two Airbus A319LR on behalf of Lufthansa on the Düsseldorf to Newark and Chicago routes. There are seats for 48 passengers in each of the two aircraft. Four supplementary fuel tanks in the freight hold provide the machines with an intercontinental range. A variant of the A319LR is the corporate jet A319CJ. There are three versions with varying take-off weights and range under completion. These have a radius of

The A319 for Air Canada during an acceptance flight.

action of up to 5000 kilometres, the A319 having the greatest range for its class.

In July 1997, Airbus Industrie made the official start on the project for a business jet, the A319CJ (Corporate Jet) which first flew on 12 November 1998. The first of these aircraft has two additional fuel tanks and more powerful engines. Most routes can be flown non-stop subject to the range limitation of 11,700 kilometres. The cabin has seating for from eight to forty passengers. An integral passenger stairway is an optional extra.

Airbus A319				
Manufacturer:	Airbus Industrie Deutschland.		Weight empty:	40,100 kgs.
Purpose:	Short and medium-distance commercial aircraft for 124 to 145 passengers.		Maximum take-off weight:	75.5 tonnes.
			Maximum landing weight:	62.5 tonnes.
Crew:	Two pilots and three to four flight attendants.		Maximum payload:	18.4 tonnes.
Engine plant:	2 x CFM International CFM56-5A/B, each rated 98 to 104 kN (10,160 to 10,500 kp) standing thrust or 2 x IAE V2500-A5 of same rating.		Maximum tank capacity:	26,760 litres.
			Maximum cruising speed:	900 kms/hr (10,050 m), 840 kms/hr (11,280 m).
			Landing speed:	230 kms/hr.
Wingspan:	34.10 m.		Service ceiling:	12500 m.
Length:	33.8 m.		Take-off run:	1900 m.
Height:	11.8 m.		Range:	6,500 kms max; 3,350 kms with full tanks and 124 passengers.
Wing area:	123 sq.m.			
Wing sweep:	25°		Fuel consumption:	2500 litres/hr.
Wing loading:	555.10 kgs/sq.m			
Fuselage diameter:	3.96 m.			

Corporate Jetliner-Version of the A319. This aircraft went to a client in India.

The Swiss Privat Air flew the A319-100 to New York on behalf of Lufthansa.

Airbus A320

Airbus Industrie announced the beginning of the A320 programme officially on 2 March 1984. The design was for a short and middle-distance aircraft for 150 to 180 passengers. It was an entirely new development, one of the few modern commercial aircraft not to be a further development or improved version of an existing model. A multitude of technical innovations was introduced into the development, particularly in the field of aerodynamics and aircraft control. The wings built at British Aerospace have a relatively small surface and a sweep of 25°. The supercritical profile provides great efficiency at high speeds. The leading edge slats extend over almost the entire wingspan and like the flaps and spoilers (five per wing) are controlled by the Fly-by-Wire System. The three tanks are integral in the wings and have a volume of 23,860 litres.

The striking livery of Swiss airline Edelweiss.

Tiger Airways of Singapore ordered several A320-200's.

The A320 was the first commercial aircraft to be fitted with fly-by-wire. The traditional control stick was replaced by a small sidestick.

The control instructions are conveyed as electrical impulses to the hydraulic regulating units for the rudder and control surfaces by means of computers through which all control instructions and data pass. The computers are so programmed that the aircraft cannot exceed its performance profile in a critical area. The removal of the mechanical and hydraulic connections enabled the achievement of a weight reduction.

The cockpit is fully digitalized and equipped with viewing screens and computers. Information is presented on six coloured, high resolution screens providing the primary flight data such as flight attitude, speed and altitude, together with data respecting navigation, engine plant and systems. As a back up conventional electro-mechanical instruments remain available for the most important data.

The A320 is a so-called narrow fuselage aircraft with a single central aisle. The fuselage had a diameter of 3.96 metres. The passenger cabin is 27.5 metres long, 3.63 metres broad and 2.2 metres high. It has seating for between 150 and 180 passengers and is equipped with a centralized entertainment system (BITE/FIDS). The holds below the cabin have a volume of

Lufthansa is numbered amongst the major operators of the A320-200.

40.8 square metres, enough room for seven LD3-46 containers.

Either CFM56-5 or International Aero Engines IAE V2500 turbines are available. The use of new metal alloys such as aluminium-lithium and modern synthetic materials resulted in great savings in weight. The entire tailplane, ailerons, spoilers and flaps are all made from compound materials.

By the time the aircraft was rolled out of the hangar on 14 February 1987, there were 262 orders and 157 options on the books for the A320. On 22 February 1987 the prototype (F-WWAI) left the runway at Toulouse for its maiden flight. This lasted three hours 23 minutes. Four aircraft were used for flight testing. The other three prototypes flew on 27 April, 18 June and 8 July 1987 while two mock-

An A320-200 of British Airways shortly before landing at Gatwick.

An A320-200 of the Portuguese airline SATA.

ups were manufactured for static stability and loading tests.

The European licence for flight with the CFM56-engines was issued on 26 February 1988. The delivery of the series production began on 28 March 1988 to Air France and British Airways three days later. The first Air France A320 entered commercial passenger service on 18 April 1988. The A320's delivered

to British Airways were ordered originally by British Caledonian; this airline had meanwhile been taken over by British Airways.

On an exhibition flight during an air show on 26 June 1988 one of the first Air France A320's in passenger service crashed into a wood near Mulhouse, Alsace. The aircraft was full but by some miracle only three persons lost their lives. The aircraft had flown over the airfield very slowly and at such low altitude that it was unable to gain sufficient height to clear the edge of the wood. This accident unleashed a heated debate about the reliability of the fly-by-wire system. The crash-site investigators ruled the cause to be pilot error, a verdict which remains disputed.

After 21 A320-100 had been built, this gave way in the autumn of 1988 to the production of the A320-200. The A320-100 has a maximum take-off weight of 66 tonnes and was equipped with CFM56-5-A1 engines. The A320-200 take-off weight is greater at 73.5 tonnes. An additional tank had been fitted inside a central wing section and winglets were added at the wing ends in order to reduce drag. The first A320-200 entered service with Ansett Australia

Until the termination of all formalities, aircraft in Spain receive a registration consisting of the country code and a three-figure number.

in November 1988. The aircraft was offered with either CFM-56 engines or the IAE V2500-A1. The first A320 flight with the latter plant took place on 28 July 1988. The licence for this combination was issued on 6 July 1989. The first client was Cyprus Airways.

Four years after entering commercial service (July 1992), the A320 worldwide has flown for

flight lasting three hours 20 minutes. The V2527-A5 intended for the A320 has a standing thrust of 118 kN. United Airlines was the first client for this version. The JAA licence for the A320 equipped with IAE V2527-5A engines was granted in August 1993. In December 1992 the 400th A320 came off the assembly line and was delivered to Northwest Airlines at the beginning of 1993. The millionth flight of an A320 took place in January 1993.

On 11 July 1993 Ansett Australia began its non-stop flights from Perth to the Christmas Islands. Ansett was the first airline to fly the A320 with the 120-minute ETOPS certificate; this covers four aircraft equipped with the CFM56-5 engine.

The 500th A320 was delivered on 20 January 1995. It went to United Airlines. In March 1998 the A320 celebrated its tenth anniversary of entering airline service. During this period the A320 family carried 517 million passengers. As the 3,000th aircraft to be completed by Airbus, on 21 July 2002 an A320 was delivered to JetBlue in the United States.

The A320-200 Enhanced has been delivered since 2008. To reduce air resistance the fuselage-wing joint was redesigned and the engine mounts modified. These measures led to a 15% saving in operating costs. The passenger cabin was gone over and given larger luggage compartments.

In August 2008 China set up a "Final Assembly Line China" (FALC) for the A320. The A320-FALC is a joint venture between Airbus, the Tianjin Free Trade Zone and the China Aviation Industry Corporation (AVIC). Airbus China holds 51% of the shares, the Chinese consortium 49%. On 18 May 2009 the first A320 completed in China made its maiden flight from Tianjin, lasting four hours 14

more than a million hours and carried around 70 million passengers. The prototype flew for the first time with the International Aero Engines V2500-A5 on 10 November 1992, the

minutes. The machine was piloted by Harry Nelson and Philippe Pellerin. Deliveries of further A319's and A320's were planned for 2009. From 2010 up to four aircraft monthly are scheduled to leave the final assembly line.

The A320 even sold well in China. Here is an A320-200 of TransAsia Airways.

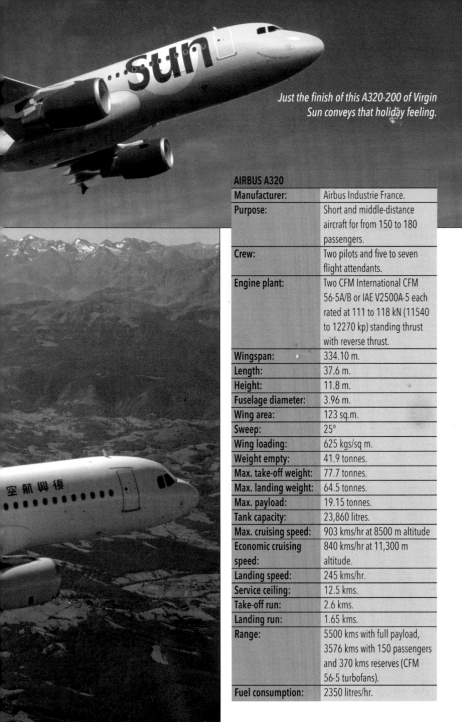

Just the finish of this A320-200 of Virgin Sun conveys that holiday feeling.

空航興復

AIRBUS A320	
Manufacturer:	Airbus Industrie France.
Purpose:	Short and middle-distance aircraft for from 150 to 180 passengers.
Crew:	Two pilots and five to seven flight attendants.
Engine plant:	Two CFM International CFM 56-5A/B or IAE V2500A-5 each rated at 111 to 118 kN (11540 to 12270 kp) standing thrust with reverse thrust.
Wingspan:	334.10 m.
Length:	37.6 m.
Height:	11.8 m.
Fuselage diameter:	3.96 m.
Wing area:	123 sq.m.
Sweep:	25°
Wing loading:	625 kgs/sq m.
Weight empty:	41.9 tonnes.
Max. take-off weight:	77.7 tonnes.
Max. landing weight:	64.5 tonnes.
Max. payload:	19.15 tonnes.
Tank capacity:	23,860 litres.
Max. cruising speed:	903 kms/hr at 8500 m altitude
Economic cruising speed:	840 kms/hr at 11,300 m altitude.
Landing speed:	245 kms/hr.
Service ceiling:	12.5 kms.
Take-off run:	2.6 kms.
Landing run:	1.65 kms.
Range:	5500 kms with full payload, 3576 kms with 150 passengers and 370 kms reserves (CFM 56-5 turbofans).
Fuel consumption:	2350 litres/hr.

Airbus A321

On 27 November 1989 Airbus Industrie announced work on the A321, a further development of the A320 belonging to the standard-fuselage family to be joined later by the A319 and A318. The A321 was designed for routes with high passenger traffic for which the A320 was too small. With its range of 4500 kms it is the ideal airliner for short and medium distance hauls. The A321 is longer than the A320 by 6.9 metres, two additional fuselage sections. The extra section ahead of the main wing is 4.27 metres, that behind it 2.63 metres. The fuselage diameter is 3.95 metres and is 19 cms broader than comparable competitors. The maximum take-off weight at 82.8 tonnes is heavier by 9.5 tonnes. This resulted in the need to reinforce numerous parts such as the wings, undercarriage and mainframes. More powerful engines were also added. Room was made for up to 220 passengers by having narrower seats. The holds have a volume of 52.2 square metres and can take five additional containers.

The wings of the four standard-fuselage aircraft are basically similar. By using a super-critical profile in which the airflow runs closely over a large section of the wing surface and disruptive vortices appear at the rear edge, the ratio of lift to air resistance in the conventional profile was greatly improved. As on the A310

This Lufthansa A321-100 D-AIRX wears the livery of the early years of the airline.

During the 2008 football World Cup, Swiss aircraft bore the legend "AIRLINE FOR ALL FANS".

the winglets at the wing-ends reduce energy loss caused by the eddying of the airflow in these regions. On the A321 too, great value was placed on an aerodynamically favourable and weight-saving method of construction. The greater savings were aimed for in the tail-plane, where 3900 kgs of carbon-fibre compound materials were employed. The weight saving as against conventional metal construction was around 800 kgs.

An Air France A321 taking off.

The aircraft is equipped with three independent hydraulic systems. Two of these are driven by pumps in the engine, the third by an electric pump. In the event of a failure in one of the systems, the required pressure will be maintained by the other two systems so that the undercarriage can be extended without problems and the rudder gear worked. If the electrical and engine systems fail simultaneously the hydraulic pressure can be maintained by an emergency generator driven by the airflow. As with the A318, A319 and A320, the A321 has fly-by-wire control. Should a failure of all systems occur it is possible to link the mechanical connections for trimming to the important control surfaces and land the aircraft.

Pilots can programme a run into the Flight Management System or call up routes from storage. Autopilot, engine and flight performance together with the vertical and horizontal flight situation of the aircraft are monitored by this system. Normally only at

Turkish Airlines Airbus A321 in the act of leaving the ground.

take-off and landing will the aircraft be piloted manually by sidestick. The main information displays are six high-resolution colour screens showing airspeed, altitude, engine, navigational and systems data and the flight attitude. The most important information is also displayed on conventional instrumentation. The data is only shown for a brief period so as not to present the pilots with an excess of information, disturbing concentration. Pilots require only one qualification for all four types, A318, A319, A320 and A321 because of the similarity of the cockpit layouts.

The final assembly of the first A321 began on 15 June 1992, and the maiden flight of the first of four prototypes went ahead on 11 March

Vietnam Airlines operates several A320-200's.

1993. The aircraft was licensed in March 1994. Production of the A321 is being undertaken at Hamburg-Finkenwerder. For the first time the partner firms Alenia and Kawasaki were co-opted to the A321 programme. Lufthansa put their first machine into service on 27 January 1994.

The A321-200, a heavier version with more powerful engines, a raised take-off weight of 89 tonnes and greater fuel capacity, can fly

This photo is history. In the 1990's the Belgian airline Sabena encountered financial turbulence and was forced to cease operations.

An Alitalia A321-100 before delivery (notice French registration marking).

A321-100	
Manufacturer:	Airbus Industrie, Germany.
Purpose:	Short and medium-haul commercial aircraft for 186-220 passengers.
Crew:	Two pilots and six to ten flight assistants.
Engine plant:	2 x IAE V2530-A5 turbofans each rated 137.8 kN (14,060 kp). CFM International CFM56-5B1 each rated 133.4 kN (13,607 kp) or 2 x CFM56-5B2 each rated 137.9 kN (14,063 kp) standing thrust and reverse thrust.
Wingspan:	33.91 m.
Length:	44.51 m.
Height:	11.76 m.
Fuselage diameter:	3.95 m.
Cabin breadth and height:	3.70 x 2.13 m resp.
Wing area:	126 sq.m.

Wing sweep:	25º
Wing loading:	671 kgs/sq.m.
Weight empty:	46,960 kgs.
Max. take-off weight:	82.2 tonnes.
Max. landing weight:	73 tonnes.
Max. payload:	23.3 tonnes.
Standard payload:	19.8 tonnes.
Tank capacity:	23,950 litres.
Max. cruising speed:	903 kms/hr at 8535 m altitude
Economic cruising speed:	828 kms/hr.
Take-off speed:	278 kms/hr.
Landing speed:	250 kms/hr.
Service ceiling:	11,900 m.
Rate of climb:	725 metres/min.
Take-off run:	2900 m.
Landing run:	2000 m.
Range:	4260 kms with full payload, 5500 kms with full tanks and 186 passengers.
Fuel consumption:	2400 litres/hr.

6400 kilometres. Its maiden flight was on 12 December 1996.

Assembly of the 100th A321 commenced at the beginning of May 1998. The aircraft was destined for Alitalia and took off on its maiden flight on 1 July 1998. Onur Air was the first holiday-airline to use the A321, and took over its first machine on 30 June 1998. Based at Istanbul, routes operated are Turkey-Western Europe and also to the Middle East. Airbus placed the first A321 in China with their delivery to Sichuan Airlines.

The A321-200IGW (Increased Gross Weight) has a higher maximum take-off weight of 93 tonnes. Spanair was the first client to place an order for this version in July 1999.

Royal Air Maroc uses the A321 for middle-distance routes.

The A330 replaced the MD-11 at KLM.

Airbus 330-200/ -300

The programmes for the twin-engine medium and long-haul A330 and for the extreme long haul four-engined A340 were begun officially in June 1987. Cockpit, fuselage wings and tailplane of both versions are practically identical. The differences lie mainly in the

number of engines and the respective systems. A330 and A340 are fitted with all the tried and tested modern technologies such as fly-by-wire sidestick, integrated display screens in the cockpit and the central maintenance system. Substantial weight savings have been achieved by the use of new working and artificial materials. The choice of engines is between the A330 GEC CF6-80E1, Pratt & Whitney PW4000 and Rolls-Royce Trent 700. The A330 and A340 are manufactured on the same production line.

This photo of Qatar's A330-200 was taken in January 2007.

An A330-200 of the Swiss national airline.

Thomas Cook is one of the holiday-flight leaders in Europe.

Two versions are being built: the basic variant A330-300, the development of which began in 1987, and the A330-200 with a greater all-up take-off weight of 230 tonnes.

The programme start for these versions was November 1995. The fuselage diameter of the A330/340 at 5.64 metres corresponds to that of the A300/30 but in contrast to the A300 the

Lufthansa accepted the forst A330-300's in 2004.

fuselage is much longer. The wings, tailplane, cockpit and the remaining sytems were all completely redesigned. As on the other Airbus models, the wings were developed at British Aerospace and have a laminary profile which in combination with the high wing extension, the large winglets and the narrow wing flaps along the total wingspan provide high efficiency. The wing has computer-operated lift flaps. This guarantees that the curvature of the wings

always has the optimal form and provides the greatest economy at all speeds. An artificial film with very fine grooves is applied to the wing to reduce frictional resistance.

The tailplane is made entirely of carbon fibre and has only 100 parts. It is around 140 kgs lighter in comparison to a metal tailplane which has approximately 2000 individual parts. The well-proven trimming tank in the stabilizer is also available. The cockpit is so

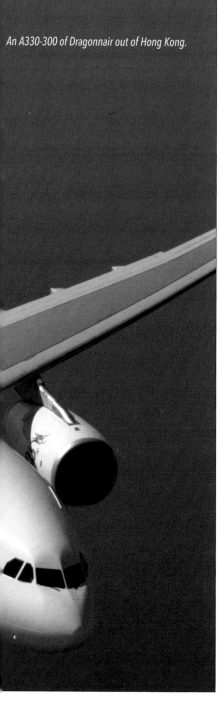

An A330-300 of Dragonnair out of Hong Kong.

standardized and typical of Airbus that pilots licensed for one type have little difficulty in converting to another. The A330-300 freight hold is the same as the A340-300. The A330 fuel tank system has a reduced capacity of 97,530 litres. The A330-300 was rolled out on 14 October 1992. About a year after the maiden flight of the A340, the A330 prototype (F-WWKA) took off on 2 November 1992 with General Electric engines in Toulouse on its first flight. This lasted four hours 55 minutes. From 29 March to 8 April 1993 experimental flights were made from high altitude airports at Khartoum and Sana. These tests took up fifty flying hours including the flight from Sana to Toulouse and were used to assess take-off and landing characteristics and survey the behaviour of engines and systems. By the end of April 1993 the two prototypes had made 173 flights totalling 516 flying hours. The third prototype wearing the colours of Air Inter which entered its flight testing programme on 28 June 1993 was the first A330 to have a completely fitted-out cabin.

In August the A330 successfully completed its first ETOPS proving flight over the North Atlantic when the machine flew six hours on one engine. From 25 August to 6 September 1993 Airbus flew distance trials with Malaysia Airlines covering 74,120 kms. On 14 October 1993 the Thai Airways International prototype fitted with Pratt & Whitney PW4168 turbofans joined the test fleet. The second prototype with PW4168 engines flew for the first time on 28 March 1994. The total flight trials lasted about 500 hours. On 31 January 1994 the prototype equipped with Rolls-Royce Trent 700 engines was flown by Nick Warner and Pierre Baud. The two test aircraft made more than 200 flights totalling over 500 flying hours. During a test

An A330-200 of the French charter company Corsair in Paris.

An A330 of the Canadian Air Transat landing at the Rhine-Main airport, Frankfurt.

flight in June 1994 an A330-300 simulating engine failure crashed. Three crew and four observers on board lost their lives. Despite this tragedy the JAA granted the licence on 22 December 1994. This also included the licence for automatic landing in poor visibility under Category III conditions. Because of the only minor differences from the A340 only a reduced programme of flight testing had to be undergone. In November the A330 was licenced for 90-minute ETOPS flights fitted with PW4164- and PW4168 engines. Up to December 1994 eight aircraft had been involved in the 1800 flying hours of flight testing.

The first orders came from Air Inter which received its A330 with GEC CF6-80E1 engines on 30 December 1993 to enter airline service in January 1994. Thai Airways ordered the aircraft with Pratt & Whitney PW4000, delivery following in August 1994. Cathay Pacific ordered Rolls Royce Trent engines and received the first aircraft on 24 February 1995.

The decision to build the A330-200 was taken on 24 November 1995. On 13 August 1997 the A330-200, works number 181, took off at Toulouse on its maiden flight lasting four hours ten minutes. Five crew were aboard, pilots being William Wainwright and Bernd Schäfer. The aircraft was fitted with two GEC CF6-80E1 engines. The second prototype with Pratt & Whitney PW4000 engines made its first flight on 4 December 1997.

The A330-200 was designed as a long-haul aircraft with 253 passengers and a range of over 12,000 kilometres. As opposed to the A330-300 the modified wing tanks hold 139,000 litres, around 41,500 litres more. The fuselage is shorter by 5.3 metres. It was necessary to enlarge the rudder gear and tailplane making the A330-200 one metre

AIRBUS A330-300	
Manufacturer:	Airbus Industrie France
Purpose:	Medium- and Long-hauls, commercial aircraft for 335 to 440 passengers
Crew:	Two pilots and eight to twelve flight attendants
Engine plant:	2 x GEC CF6-80E1, Pratt & Whitney PW4164/PW4168 or Rolls Royce Trent 700 with 285-316 kN (29,400 to 32,500 kp) standing thrust with reverse thrust.
Wingspan:	60.30 m.
Length:	63.70 m.
Height:	16.80 m.
Fuselage diameter:	5.64 m.
Wing area:	362 sq.m.
Sweep:	30°
Wing loading:	585.60 kgs/sq.m.
Weight empty:	124.1 tonnes.
Max. take-off weight:	230 tonnes.
Max. landing weight:	185 tonnes.
Max. payload:	43.5 tonnes.
Max. tank capacity:	97,530 litres.
Max. cruising speed:	945 kms/hr.
Economic cruising speed:	861 kms/hr at 11,890 m altitude.
Landing speed:	260 kms/hr.
Service ceiling:	12,500 m.
Rate of climb:	750 m/min.
Take-off run:	3000 m.
Landing run:	2000 m.
Range:	7500 km with full payload or 8900 kms with full tanks and 335 passengers.
Fuel consumption:	6500 litres/hr.

higher than the basic version. Flight testing lasted 630 hours. On 21 March 1998 the A330-200 set a world speed record on the flight from Toulouse to Santiago with an average speed of 890 kms/hr.

On 31 March 1998 the European JAA, the US FAA and Transport Canada all awarded the type its licence simultaneously. At this time the A330-200 had flown 380 hours on 169 flights. On 29 April 1998 the first machine went to Canada 3â000, which leased it from ILFC. It has GEC CF6-80E1A4 engines. With these engines before delivery the A330-200 received the 180-minute ETOPS certificate from the JAA and Transport Canada. The A330-200 is the first aircraft in aviation history to receive simultaneously the type-licence from the joint European licensing authority JAA, the Federal Aviation Administration FAA and Transport Canada.

The A330-200 fitted with Pratt & Whitney PW4000 engines received the JAA licence on 13 July 1998 after a total of 129 test flights: the maiden flight with Rolls Royce Trent 700 engines took place on 24 June 1998, the licence being awarded at the end of 1998 after 100 flying hours.

Airbus A340-200/ -300

In 1976 Airbus Industrie introduced for the first time the design for a four-engined long-haul commercial aircraft, the A300-B11, with a planned range of around 10,000 kilometres. The design was then revised and in 1980 a totally new aircraft appeared in three versions. The TA9 was a twin-jet short-haul machine for 320 passengers, the four-jet TA11 had a capacity of up to 235 passengers and a range of 12,000 kilometres and the TA12 was a twin-jet long distance aircraft. As already mentioned about the A330, both programmes, for the A330 and A340, were begun officially on 5 June 1987. Four European countries are involved in the Airbus programme. These are Aerospatiale/France (37.9% share), EADS/Germany (37.9%), British Aerospace (20%) and EADS/CASA of Spain (4.2%). Aerospatiale delivers the nose section and cockpit, the mountings for the engine gondolas and a section of the central fuselage. Aerospatiale is also responsible for the final assembly.

EADS completes the greater part of the fuselage, the rudder gear and the cabin installation, British Aerospace the main wings, and EADS/CASA the tailplane.

This photograph gives an impression of the size of an A340-200.

A340-200 of the Austrian above the Alps.

In contrast to the two-jet A330, only the CFM56-5C engines of CFM International are offered for the four-engined A340 with an air intake enlarged by 10.2 cms. Initially the CFM56-5C2 with 139 kN (14,150 kp) was installed. An IAE engine was intended as an option, but the development of the engine was abandoned by the manufacturer.

The A330 and A340 are essentially similar in build, including the wings. The A340 wings were given local reinforcement in the region of the two outer engines.

Because the A340 is used on long-distance flights of over 16 hours it has more crew. For off-duty pilots there is a rest room behind the cockpit. A rest area with six places for the flight attendants is located in the rear loading bay accessible by a spiral stairway.

The A340 is equipped with a central flight monitoring system. The central servicing computer maintains details of all on-board systems and monitors their condition. It has the ability to identify various malfunctions and locate their origins. Furthermore, after landing the computer automatically provides a condition report on the aircraft which speeds up and simplifies maintenance.

From the beginning of planning onwards two versions of the A340 were envisaged: the A340-200 for ultra-long distances and 261 passengers, and the 4.2-metre longer A340-300 with a capacity for 295 passengers.

The Aerodynamiker 20 models, wingspan up to 6 metres and two tonnes in weight, were tested in ten different European wind tunnels. This required a total of 3000 working days. In August 1990 Deutsche Airbus delivered the first wing to Toulouse. This came from British Aerospace and was completed fully equipped at Bremen. In December 1990 the first major

The veneer of Royal Jordanian aircraft provides a very elegant appearance.

The colourful livery of Air Jamaica aircraft contrasts strongly with the monotonous paintwork of many other airlines.

component parts of the A340, a nose section and central fuselage section arrived for final assembly. The four CFM56-5C2 engines were installed into the A340 mainframe in April 1991.

The first A340-300 rolled out of the hangar on 4 October 1991. The maiden flight ensued on 25 October 1991 and lasted five hours. Pilot was Chief Test Pilot Pierre Baud. The A340-200 took off on its maiden flight on 3 February 1992. The fourth prototype had a fully fitted cabin and flew for the first time on 15 June 1992.

For flight testing six aircraft were used making 750 flights and clocking up 2400 flying hours. Testing was done in three phases. In the first phase the attitude of the aircraft at all speeds and altitudes; next the loss of the various systems was tested. In the the third phase flight data and the flying attitude were examined with the aircraft iced up, and the navigation installation checked.

The fly-by-wire control system was coordinated with the the four engines. The first two new flight regulator computers, the flight management and guidance computer FMGC and the flight contriol unit FCU, were delivered by Sextant Avionique in November 1990. Both are part of the auto-flight system.

Before and during flight testing, static tests were made overloading an airframe until it collapsed. Fatigue tests were carried out on a second unit in which the aircraft was exposed to a loading two and a half times heavier than normal. Component parts of special importance for safety must be proven to last five times the stated lifetime.

An A340-200 landed at Perth, Australia on 23 October 1992 having flown the Toulouse-

The A340-300 are amongst the largest aircraft in the Olympic Airways fleet.

Perth leg (15,000 kms) in sixteen hours 22 minutes. Flight testing was concluded on 22 December 1992 with the award of the JAA licence.

The first series aircraft, an A340-200 of Lufthansa, made its initial flight on 7 December 1992; it was handed over on 29 January 1993 and accepted into passenger service on the Frankfurt-Newark run on 15 March. The first machine of the A340-300 series flew for the first time on 15 January 1993 and was transferred to Air France on 26 February. It was

the 1000th aircraft to be delivered by Airbus. The type was awarded the FAA licence on 27 May 1993.

The Airbus A340-200 "World Ranger" took off on 18 June 1993 from Paris for a round-the-world flight. It was the first passenger aircraft to achieve this feat with only one stop. It was also the longest-ever flight by a passenger aircraft. The circumnavigation took 48 hours 22 minutes. The stretch between Paris and Auckland was flown in 21 hours 46 minutes.

Emirates, main office at Dubai, operates a large fleet of Airbus aircraft.

On 14 March 1994 the licence was issued for the CFM56-5C3 rated at 145 kN (14,800 kp). A year later on 17 March the more powerful CFM56-5C4 rated at 151 kN (15,410 kp) was also licensed. The first operator of A340 with CFM56-5C4 was Kuwait Airways. The 100th A340 went to Singapore Airlines on 1 March 1997.

From April 1995 Airbus Industrie offered the A340-8000. This was a variant of the A340-200 with greater range. It could fly 14,800 kms with 232 passengers. Two additional tanks were fitted, the maximum take-off weight being 285.1 tonnes. Maiden flight was in December 1997, delivery the following year.

In 2003 Airbus Industrie began developing the improved A340-300E (Enhanced) which included many technical innovations from the A340-500 and -600. The mechanical controls are discarded in favour of the fly-by-wire electronic system creating space in the rear of the fuselage for a rest room with eight beds for off-duty crew members. Propulsion is provided by four CFM56-5C4/P engines each

Air Canada has operated A340-300 C-FYLG since May 1987.

A British West Indies A340-300 landing at Zurich.

rated 151 kN with notably low fuel consumption, lower maintenance costs and longer life. Cockpit design was based on the A340-500 and -600 and the passenger cabin modernized. The aircraft was rolled out in October 2003. At the beginning of 2004 the A340-300E's were delivered to the first airlines ordering them, South African Airways and Swiss. Once the A340-300E began completing, production of the earlier versions was abandoned. The new version has some improvements.

AIRBUS A340-300		
Manufacturer:	Airbus Industrie France.	
Purpose:	Long haul commercial airliner for 295-440 passengers.	
Engine plant:	4 x CFM International CFM56-5C2 each rated 139-151 kN (14,175-15,400 kp) standing thrust with reverse thrust.	
Wingspan:	60.30 m.	
Length:	63.70 m.	
Height:	16.8 m.	
Fuselage diameter:	5.64 m.	
Wing area:	362 sq.m.	
Sweep:	30°	

Weight empty:	130.2 tonnes.	
Max. take-off weight:	275 tonnes.	
Max. landing weight:	190 tonnes.	
Max. payload:	43.5 tonnes.	
Max. tank capacity:	148,700 litres.	
Max. cruising speed:	914 kms/hr at 10,060 m altitude	
Economic cruising speed:	880 kms/hr at 11,890 m altitude.	
Service ceiling:	12,500 m.	
Range:	13,500 kms with full tanks and 295 passengers.	

An A340-500 of Qatar Airways.

Airbus A340-500/ -600

On 8 December 1997 Airbus Industrie gave the green light for the new A340-500/-600. At this time there were already provisional contracts and declarations of intent on the table for around 100 aircraft from seven airlines. Lufthansa was the first client actively involved in the development of the new Airbus A340-600. The new variants led to a multitude of technical modifications in comparison to the standard A340.

Despite all innovations and improvements with the A3340-600 it was an important factor

High above the clouds an A340-500 of Air Canada.

that both the A340-300 and the A340-600 could be flown with the same licence. The cockpit was almost unchanged except for the components necessary for an aircraft the size of the A340-600. As a result lengthy and expensive conversion training was hardly necessary. For conversion from the A340-300 to the A340-500 and -600 a maximum of only six hours' theoretical training is needed.

The A340-500 has six more cross-frames than the A340-300 and can seat 313 passengers. Range is 15,750 kilometres. The aircraft has additional tanks for 214,810 litres. The freight holds can take up to 31 LD-3 containers.

The A340-600, for the same fuselage cross-

Lufthansa put ten A340-600's into service.

section as the A340-300, was lengthened by twenty cross-frames, eleven in the forward part, three in the centre and six in the rear of the machine, giving the aircraft an extra 11.1 metres for an overall length of 74.8 metres. Thus the A340-600 is the longest passenger aircraft in the world. This, and the increased weight, required modifications to the fuselage for increased stresses. There is room for 43 LD-3 containers in the underfloor freight rooms. The machine is designed for 380 passengers and has a range of 13,900 kilometres. The wingspan was increased by 3.5 metres to 63.5 metres. The wing depth was also increased so that the wing area was enlarged by 20% to

437.3 square metres. A new wing bunker running the length of the wingspan raised the fuel capacity to 195,620 litres. The 1-metre higher rudder came from the A330-200. The stabilizer has a wingspan of 23 metres and a surface area of almost 100 square metres. 8000 litres of fuel is carried inside it.

The undercarriage and brakes were made substantially larger. The unbraked two-wheel chassis below the fuselage was replaced by a four-wheel unit, which now has a braking system, to help contain the extra take-off weight. All fourteen wheels of the nose and main undercarriage together take about 100 tonnes more than previously, of which the new

A340-600 in the new livery of Thai Airways International.

"central" undercarriage takes a substantial proportion.

The distance between the nose and main chassis was increased to 33 metres, eight metres longer than on the A340-300. The pilots are seated about seven metres ahead of the nose wheels which are used to steer the aircraft on the ground. This requires an additional support which is supplied by the Taxi Aid Camera System (TACS), consisting of two video cameras, one installed on the rudder and one below the rear fuselage section.

The camera on the rudder is aligned obliquely downwards and shows the entire fuselage. It also provides a view of the runway and both outer elements of the main landing gear. The camera below the fuselage shows the position of the nose wheels. These cameras transmit to a screen in the cockpit so that the pilots can see how and to where the aircraft is rolling. There are also additional markings faded in to aid in the touch down of the nose wheels.

The air conditioning system in the A340-600 had to be adjusted for the greater number of passengers. Modifications have led to a better individual regulation of the cabin micro-climate to improve air supply to the window seats. Air circulation and temperature control is better without raised noise levels. For the first time it is also possible to suit air requirements to passenger numbers. Also new is the lighting technology in the cabin. There is a choice of 64 different lighting fitments easy to operate by the flight attendants. The Rolls Royce Trent 500 with a standing thrust of 249 kN (25,400 kp) was selected for the engine plant. This engine is a development of the Trent 700/800 already in service with the A330 and the Boeing 777.

On 23 April 2001 the A340/600 (c/n 360) took off from Toulouse on a testing flight which lasted five hours 22 minutes. The second machine (c/n 371) flew on 8 June 2001 and was used to test systems, the autopilot and the transmission of engine data while the third A340-600 (c/n 376) with a fully equipped

passenger cabin was integrated into the flight testing programme in September 2001.

The A340-500 made its maiden flight on 11 February 2002. Piloted by Airbus Chief Test Pilot Jacque Rosay, co-pilot Richard Monnoy, assisted by flight engineers Didier Ronoeray, Bruno Bigand and Sylvie Loisel-Lebate, this flight lasted five hours 52 minutes. This was the first time that an Airbus aircraft on its maiden flight had had a female crew member aboard.

The machine had a take-off weight of 280 tonnes of which 30.5 tonnes was test instrumentation. Two aircraft flew for 340 hours for the A340-500 flight tests. The aircraft was licensed on 3 December 2002 by the JAA (Joint Aviation Authority). Shortly afterwards the first aircraft were delivered to Air Canada. On 8 April 2002 an A340-600 took off from London Heathrow within the framework of the licensing programme for two-week long route trials with Lufthansa and Virgin Atlantic crews. 17 airports

An A340-600 in the colours of the Chinese airline Chinese Eastern.

A340-600's are used on South African Airways' long haul flights.

A340-500/-600's differ from the A340-200/-300 series by their larger engines. Here a machine of Singapore Airlines is seen taking off.

were visited. The JAA issued the passenger licence on 29 May 2002. Three A340-600 took part in the licensing programme which involved more than 500 flights lasting a total of 1600 flying hours.

Virgin Atlantic as first customer confirmed its provisional order for eight A340-600 to be delivered in 2002. Virgin Atlantic planned innovations for the A340-600 such as separate cabins with double beds in the forward under-floor area, a bar/lounge, casino, showers and a fitness/ massage room in the rear under-floor area. The first machine was accepted in July 2002 for routes in the United States. In July 2003 Airbus Industry delivered its 500th aircraft of the A330/340 family. This was the A340-600 to be operated by Cathay Pacific.

As Lufthansa had no need of the extra space gained by lengthening the aircraft, a large kitchen was installed in the lower deck to cook for 160 passengers and five washrooms for the Economy Class, making way for 25 extra seats in the newly arranged main deck in the upper section of the aircraft. As against the A340-300

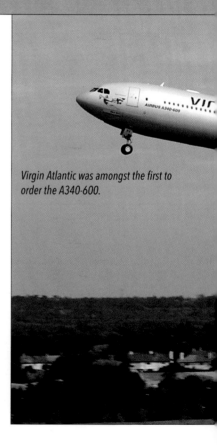

Virgin Atlantic was amongst the first to order the A340-600.

there is room for another 100 passengers. The two decks are connected by an 80-cm wide stairway. Between the service point on the main deck and the galley in the lower deck a lift is installed for the food trolleys. Headroom on the lower deck is 1.95 metres. The second kitchen is at the rear of the machine on the main deck, as are the First and Business Class washrooms. On extremely long hauls there is a mobile rest compartment for crew members located immediately behind the underfloor galley. It is equipped with four double-tiered bunks, a total of eight beds each two metres long. In December 1997 Lufthansa submitted orders for ten A340-600's. These aircraft were delivered between July 2003 and May 2004.

On 18 November 2005 the A340-600HGW underwent flight testing. It is being delivered from 2006 and has a raised take-off weight of 376 tonnes and more powerful engines. Parts

This A340-500 of the Portuguese airline TAM is seen landing at Frankfurt after a flight from Brazil.

Qatar Airways uses both the A340-500 and A340-600.

of the fuselage and undercarriage were strengthened. A new variant of the A340-500 became available from October 2005 with a take-off weight of 380 tonnes and a range of 16,670 kilometres. The A340-300, -500 and -600 were all completed in parallel on the final assembly line at Toulouse. The production hangars there have a capacity for between six and eight aircraft monthly.

AIRBUS A340-600		Cabin length:	60.95 m
Manufacturer:	Airbus Industrie France	Weight empty:	177 tonnes.
Purpose:	Long haul passenger aircraft for 380 in typical three-class arrangement.	Max. take-off weight:	365 tonnes.
		Max. landing weight:	254 tonnes.
		Max. payload:	62.3 tonnes.
Crew:	Two pilots.	Tank capacity:	195,620 litres.
Engine plant:	4 x Rolls Royce Trent 556 each rated 249 kN (25,380 kp) standing thrust.	Max. cruising speed:	930 kms/hr.
		Economic cruising speed:	890 kms/hr.
Wingspan:	63.6 m (with winglets).	Service ceiling:	12,500 m.
Length:	74.8 m.	Take-off run:	385 m.
Height:	17.29 m.	Rate of climb to 10,850 m:	21 mins.
Wing area:	437.30 sq.m.		
Sweep:	31.1º	Range:	13,875 kms.
Fuselage diameter:	5.64 m.		

Airbus A350

The newest long-haul Airbus development is the A350, designed to introduce a new aircraft family with medium passenger capacity and an especially wide fuselage.

The first planned version presented in 2004 was a twin-jet machine for long or ultra-long hauls. The design was based on the A330 with new engines. The EADS monitoring committee decided on 10 December 2004 to allow negotiations for sales to the airlines. The official release for development work on the A350 came on 6 October 2005. By that stage 140 airlines had decided in favour of the A350. By 17 July 2006 the order book had 182 aircraft. Initially two versions were proposed, the A350-800 and -900 corresponding in their dimensions to the A330

This is how the A350 XWB should look.

and A340-200/300 which would also replace the A350.

For the engine plant, modified versions of the General Electric GENx and the Rolls Royce Trent were planned, the first protoype would fly in 2009, delivery of the series aircraft to follow in 2011.

Although the airlines ordered the A350, they were not sparing of their criticism of it and Airbus decided on fundamental changes to the concept. The airlines wanted above all a broader fuselage. The fuselage cross-section of the A350 design was the same as the A300 of the 1970s. The new variant was designated A350 XWB (XWB=Extra Wide Body) and first displayed on 17 July 2006 at the Farnborough air show. It was now only 10% A330 while the cockpit matched that of the A380. Airbus negotiated the transfer of their orders to the A350 XWB with the airlines which had ordered the first

The A350-800 version for 270 passengers.

version of the A350 and in nearly all cases the response was positive. Accordingly on 1 December 2006 EADS gave the green light to go ahead with the A350 XWB.

The A350-800 variant is offered in three basic versions: the A350-800 with a length of 60.5 metres which can carry 270 passengers in three classes over distances of up to 15,750 kilometres: th A350-900 with 314 seats and a length of 66.8 metres, and the A350-1000 with

375 seats and a length of 73.8 metres. The latter two versions have a range of 15,400 kilometres. All three versions have a cruising speed of Mach 0.85. Also planned is the A350-900R with a range of 19,000 kilometres and the freighter A350-900F. The first version to be available will be the A350-900, its maiden flight being scheduled for mid-2011. Delivery to the first clients will follow in mid-2012. The dates were put back by about a year in the course of

China Airlines is one of the companies to place orders.

development so that the A350-900 should now enter service in mid-2013. Delivery dates for the A350-800 are planned for the spring of 2014 and for the A350-1000 the beginning of 2015. The A350-900R and -900F should follow a year later. The A350 will be assembled at Toulouse.

The elliptical fuselage has a cross-section of 5.9 metres. The A350 XWB will have the broadest fuselage of the class. More than 60% of the airframe is made of new materials.

A large part of the fuselage skin is carbon fibre compound (CFK) which brings with it a

The fuselage consists of several sections with aluminium framing to which carbon-fibre compound panels have been applied. Each fuselage section has four panels, one above, one below and one to each side. If the fuselage is damaged, these can be exchanged easily.

The almost noise-free passenger cabin has larger windows and so-called "mood lighting" in which the cabin is lit in various colours simulating daylight. The cabin offers more headroom and the overhead luggage lockers have been made more accessible. There are nine or ten seats in each row across. Above the passenger cabin is the restroom for the crew; this is reached by a small stairway.

The cockpit is fitted out as a two-man glass cockpit with six liquid-crystal display screens; flight control is by sidestick. There are two head-up displays and a representation of the altitude profile flown.

The A350 XWB wings are a new design. They are of carbon-fibre reinforced artificial material allowing a weight saving of 4.5 tonnes. They are swept 35° for an optimal speed of Mach 0.85. The wing ends flow into winglets.

In contrast to the first design, newly developed Rolls Royce turbofan jets provisionally designated Trent XWB with a thrust of 34,05 kgs and 43,130 kgs have been installed. At the moment General Electric is not ready to develop an alternative. In the future engines might be forthcoming for the A350-800, but not the A350-1000, where Boeing has orders for the Boeing 777-300ER in this performance class. Airbus is looking for a second manufacturer. This might be the Engine Alliance, an offshoot of General Electric, or Pratt & Whitney, but so far nothing has been decided. Fuel is carried in three tanks. A

arge saving in weight and is also favourable for the maintenance and repair of the ndividual airframe components. Other weight-saving materials are the increasingly used aluminium-lithium alloys and so-called "Glare", a glass fibre reinforced aluminium.

There are in all around 500 orders for all versions of the A350.

trimming tank such as was first introduced on the A310 is not planned for.

On 21 December 2004 the Spanish airline Air Europa was the first client to sign a declaration of intent for ten A350-800's.

In June 2005 Qatar Airways decided on the purchase of up to sixty Airbus A350-800/900. The order was increased on 15 March 2007 to

total of eighty machines, these being twenty A350-800, twenty A350-1000 and forty A350-900. The purchase contract was signed on 18 June 2007. As the first client for the A350 XWB

Singapore Airlines announced on 21 July 2006 that it had ordered twenty A350-900 XWB's and had an option for an additional twenty. The contract to purchase was signed in June 2007.

The A350 will supersede the A330.

An A350 in the livery of Tunisair.

Beforehand at the end of December 2006, the American leasing firm Pegasus signed a contract for two A350 XWB. On 11 November 2007 Emirates ordered fifty A350-900 XWB and twenty A350-1000 XWB. On 15 September 2008 Air Caraibes ordered three A350-1000 with an arrangement for 440 passengers in three classes. Up to December 2009 there were orders for a total of 505 A350's of all versions.

AIRBUS A350-900 XWB		Length:	66.9 m.
Manufacturer:	Airbus Industrie France.	Height:	16.9 m.
Purpose:	Long distance passenger aircraft for 314 passengers in typical three-class arrangement.	Wing area:	443 sq.m.
		Sweep:	31.9° (inner) 35° (centre).
		Fuselage diameter:	5.96 m.
Crew:	Two pilots and cabin staff.	Max. take-off weight:	268 tonnes.
Engine plant:	2 x Rolls Royce Turbofan Trent XWB jets each rated 370 kN (37,713 kp) standing thrust.	Max. landing weight:	202.5 tonnes.
		Tank capacity:	150,000 litres.
		Cruising speed:	890 kms/hr.
Wingspan:	64.75 m.	Range:	15,000 kms.

Flying display of an A380 at the Aerosalon 2007, Paris-Le Bourget.

Airbus A380

The A380-800 was present at the 2008 Farnborough Air Show.

In the 1980's Airbus made the first feasibility studies for a long range aircraft. During this phase the project was designated A3XX. As a result of the increasing demand for long range aircraft in the mid-1990s and the hesitant attitude of Boeing to further develop its 747, Airbus saw the chances for their own development as good. The interest of the airlines was strong and in the year 2000 there were already fifty declarations of intent to purchase. The construction of a double-floored long haul aircraft was technical virgin territory for the European aviation industry.

Technologically, the A380 was and is a great challenge. It is the biggest passenger airline in the world: the fuselage is 2.33 metres longer than the Boeing 747-400 and the wingspan is

15.36 metres longer at 79.80 metres. Against modern long haul aircraft the A380 is c̶ ̶ ̶ more economic. Fuel consumption is lowe three litres per kilometre and passenger, anu therefore 12% below the consumption of a Boeing 747-400.

Two versions were planned initially, the passenger version A380-800 and the freighter A380-800F. Because of technical problems which led to delays in the passenger version, the freighter was held back and the entire development potential concentrated on the airliner.

In manufacture, fibre compounds were used on a large scale, amongst them "Glare", a compound material made from several layers of glass fibre and aluminium. Glare was used for the outer skin of almost the whole fuselage. Only the fuselage underside is of aluminium.

The A380 is a four-jet low-wing long-haul ⁻craft with two uniform passenger decks. The fuselage is of oval cross-section with a breadth of 7.17 metres and a height of 8.4 metres. The cockpit is placed between the main and upper decks but is entered from the main deck. For security reasons the cockpit is separated from the cabin by a bullet proof and ram-proof door. Equipped with the most up-to-date avionics and an onboard maintenance terminal (OMT), through which there is access to all important manuals and logs, it is one of the so-called "paperless" cockpits.

The passenger cabin is 50.68 metres long. In the upper deck the rows have eight passenger

seats each and ten in the main deck. Both decks are connected by two staircases and two dumb waiters. Right below is the freight deck with capacity for 38 LD-3 freight containers. The wings are of aluminium alloy and at their ends have tips 2.3 metres high of compound materials which help reduce air resistance.

Six leading edge slats of Thermoplast were fitted in the outer area of the wings both sides. On the rear of the wing are three split flaps with a total surface of 120 sq.m. The fuel tanks are integral in the wings and hold 310,000 litres.

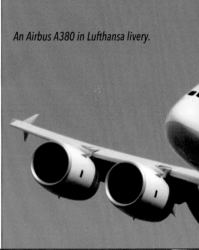
An Airbus A380 in Lufthansa livery.

An A380 prototype with Rolls Royce Trent 900 engines during a test flight with alternative fuel.

The tailplane is made completely of carbon-fibre reinforced material. The wingspan of the tailplane is 30 metres. Each rudder is operated hydraulically. There is an additional 18,600-litre fuel tank in the tail which automatically regulates the centre of gravity.

There is a choice of Rolls Royce or Engine Alliance engines each rated at 311 kN (31,750 kp). Engine Alliance is part of the General Electric/Pratt & Whitney consortium. The supercharger has a diameter of 2.95 metres.

The auxiliary Pratt & Whitney Canada PW980A generator at the rear is rated at 1470 kW and provides current for the hydraulic and electrical systems and to start up the main engines. In the extremely unlikely event that all engines should fail in flight, there is a propellor-driven ramjet for emergency power supply. The 70 kW generated is sufficient to maintain the essential instruments and equipment operational.

The landing chassis consists of a twin-wheeled gear at the nose and a main chassis

with four units, of which two units of six wheels each are housed in the central wing box at the centre of the fuselage, and two other units each with four wheels at the rear wing-crossbeam.

The production of all components is distributed amongst the various European Airbus factories and then brought to Toulouse for final assembly either by Type A330-600ST Beluga freight carriers, on heavy road transporters or by ship. Interior fitments and painting are done at Hamburg-Finkenwerder.

Machines for delivery to airlines in Europe and the Middle East are transferred from Finkenwerder, the others from Toulouse.

The A380 programme was commenced at Nantes on 23 January 2002. Four prototypes were built. The final assembly of the MSN 001 was begun in October 2004 and finished in January 2005. On 18 January that year the first A380 was shown to the public.The first prototype with the registration F-WWOW made its maiden flight from Toulouse-Blagnac on 27

Virgin Atlantic is still awaiting delivery of the A380.

April 2005. With a maximum take-off weight of 421 tonnes it was the heaviest ever passenger aircraft at the time. Engine plant was Rolls Royce Trent 970's. Flight crew were Chief Test Pilot Capt. Jacques Rosay, Flight Capt. Claude Lelaie and engineers Fernando Alonso, Gérard Desbois, Manfred Birnfeld and Jacky Joye. The aircraft touched down at Toulouse three hours 54 minutes later. MSN 009 (F-WWEA) flew for the first time on 24

August 2006 with Engine Alliance GP7200 turbines.

In parallel to the four prototypes for flight testing a mock-up, the non-flyable MSN 5001, was built for stress tests at IABG Dresden. These tests were carried out from September 2005 to 2008 in a hangar specially built for the purpose. In the fatigue experiment 47,500 flight cycles were simulated corresponding to 25 years' operational service. In another stress mock-up a

Toulouse, on 16 February 2006 cracks appeared in a wing between the engine gondolas. These cracks appeared after passing the 1.5 times maximum load. The problem was cured by additional strips to the longitudinal frame.

In July and August 2006 at the German Centre for Air and Space Travel (DLR), Oberpfaffenhofen, turbulence testing was carried out. The test results provided the minimum distance for a following aircraft. In order to have a comparison of size, the A380 alternated in overflying a Lufthansa Boeing 747-400 at a height between 80 and 400 metres above the Oberpfaffenhofen airfield. The tests showed that for taking off and landing only – depending on the sizes of the respective aircraft – greater distances had to be kept away from the A380.

Great emphasis was laid on the ability to evacuate the aircraft quickly in an emergency.

Air France accepted delivery of its first A380 in the autumn of 2009.

Computer graphic of an A380 of Etihad Airlines.

This computer graphic shows an A380 in the old Thai livery.

Existing international regulations state that it must be possible to evacuate an aircraft within 90 seconds through half the available doors. This evacuation test was carried out at Hamburg on 26 March 2006 when 853 passengers and 20 crew evacuated the aircraft through the emergency doors on the starboard side within 78 seconds.

The first flights with passengers aboard were made between 4 and 8 September 2006. The passengers were Airbus workers, 474 per flight. In November route trials were held which took the A380 halfway around the world. The licensing programme was concluded on 30 November 2006 with a flight from Vancouver to Toulouse over the North Pole.

On 12 December 2006 the A380-800 with Rolls Royce Trent 900 engines was awarded the type-licence by the European Agency for Flight Safety (EASA) and the FAA.

In mid-March 2007 an A380 flew 483 passengers in accordance with requirements from Frankfurt to Chicago via New York and from Toulouse to Los Angeles. EASA issued the

type licence for the A380 with Engine Alliance GP7200 engines on 23 April 2007.

Delivery of the A380 to Singapore Airlines was initially planned for June 2006. Because of production problems this was set back to 15 October 2007 when the airline accepted its first A380 at Toulouse. Ten days later it was put into service on the Singapore-Sydney route. In 2008 as planned, Airbus delivered twelve machines, amongst them another five to Singapore Airlines. The first, delivered from Hamburg, was the MSN 011, accepted on 28 July 2008 by Emirates.

Qantas received its first A380, the MSN 014, on 19 September 2008. At the Dubai air show on 13 November 2007 an A380 in a VIP-version was sold to Prince Al-Walid ibn Talal Al Saud. Air France KLM was the first European airline to accept its first A380 on 30 October 2009. The delivery to Lufthansa was postponed to the summer of 2010. As at November 2009 there are 202 orders for the A380-800, of which 21 machines have been delivered.

Singapore Airlines was the first airline to receive the A380.

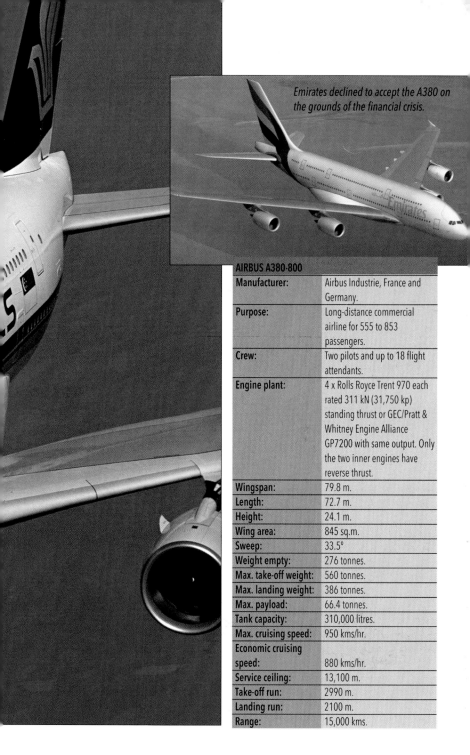

Emirates declined to accept the A380 on the grounds of the financial crisis.

AIRBUS A380-800

Manufacturer:	Airbus Industrie, France and Germany.
Purpose:	Long-distance commercial airline for 555 to 853 passengers.
Crew:	Two pilots and up to 18 flight attendants.
Engine plant:	4 x Rolls Royce Trent 970 each rated 311 kN (31,750 kp) standing thrust or GEC/Pratt & Whitney Engine Alliance GP7200 with same output. Only the two inner engines have reverse thrust.
Wingspan:	79.8 m.
Length:	72.7 m.
Height:	24.1 m.
Wing area:	845 sq.m.
Sweep:	33.5°
Weight empty:	276 tonnes.
Max. take-off weight:	560 tonnes.
Max. landing weight:	386 tonnes.
Max. payload:	66.4 tonnes.
Tank capacity:	310,000 litres.
Max. cruising speed:	950 kms/hr.
Economic cruising speed:	880 kms/hr.
Service ceiling:	13,100 m.
Take-off run:	2990 m.
Landing run:	2100 m.
Range:	15,000 kms.

The first A400M being rolled-out at Seville, October 2008.

Airbus Military A400M

Belgium, Germany, France, Great Britain, Italy, Spain and Turkey were the nations making the decision for the A400M military transport aircraft. The agreement was made at the Paris-Le Bourget Aerosalon when the seven States signed the preliminary contract for the development and construction of the A400M. This aircraft would replace the Lockheed C-130 Hercules and the Transall C-160 in each of the individual air forces from 2007. There were actually eight nations planning to accept 196

A400M's. The contracts were to be distributed as follows: seven aircraft for the Belgian Air Force (from 2018), 73 for Germany (from 2009), 50 for France (from 2008), 25 for Great Britain (from 2008), three for Portugal (from 2016), 27 for Spain (from 2010) and ten for Turkey (from 2008). Italy was to have received 15 A400M, but at the end of 2001 left the common development and decided to acquire more Lockheed C-130J Hercules and Alenia C-27J Spartans. Luxemburg applied for one machine to be delivered in 2013.

It was as early as 1982 that Aérospatiale, British Airspace, Lockheed and MBB gave initial consideration to a successor for the Hercules and the Transall, designating it FIMA (Future

The A400M was to replace the Transall C-160D in the German Bundeswehr.

International Military Airlifter). The transporter would carry a useful payload of twenty to thirty tonnes and have a range of around 4500 kms. In 1985 eight European Governments set up a working group for the project now entitled "FLA" (Future Large Aircraft). In 1987 when Alenia/Italy and CASA/Spain resigned from the FIMA consortium, Lockheed also left the

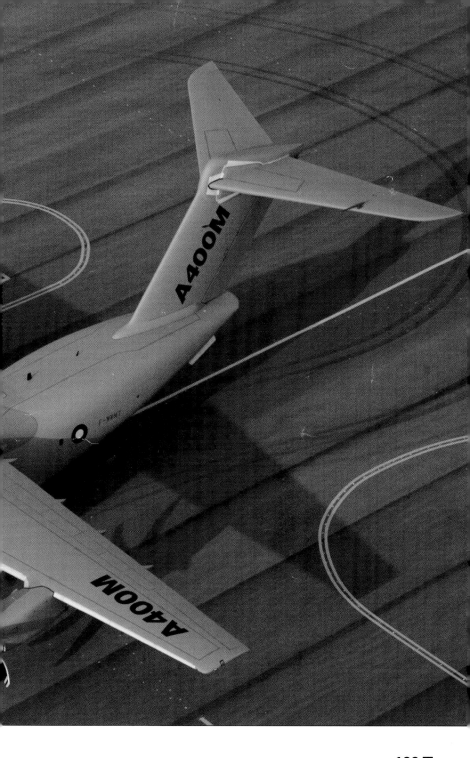

To date nine nations have placed orders for the aircraft.

France is responsible for the ramp at the rear and the cockpit as well as the integration of the flight control system.

The wings are made in Great Britain and Germany (wing sheeting). The flaps, leading edge slats and coverings are made by Flabel/Belgium, TAI/Turkey and in Spain. CASA

is responsible for the elevator gear and engine housing and handles the final assembly with San Pablo/Seville.

The development of the A400M was based on the experience gained by Airbus Industrie from its civilian models, and includes fly-by-wire, modern wing aerodynamics and the use

of compound substances such as carbon fibre reinforced plastic for the fuselage centre section and the wing covering. The cockpit is based on the A340 with additional military instrumentation. Seven exchangeable multi-function displays (MFD's) have been allowed for, amongst them the primary flight display PFD and a navigational screen which will provide a ground display incorporating known danger areas. The cockpit has two head-up displays to provide primary flight data and will be used for night-sight equipment. For the first time the A400M as a new military airlifter will be equipped with Sidestick. Also in automatic engine control (Full-authority Digital Engine Control FADEC), Airbus aircraft rely on proven technology which as here monitor the flight parameters by means of fully electronic handling. The cockpit windscreens and seats are armoured to offer protection against projectiles of up to 12.7mm. The fuselage length of 42.2 metres is longer than the Hercules and the Transall. The highest point of the aircraft at the tip of the rudder is 14.7 metres. The freight box 3.85 metres high and 4 metres wide, has a volume of 356 cubic metres and can take a useful load of 37 tonnes. The cabin floor is 17.71 metres long and the loading ramp 5.4 metres long. Capacity is for nine 88 x 108-inch containers. A crane with a lifting capacity of five tonnes can be installed in the freight room for self-loading.

Up to six Landrovers with trailers, two attack helicopters, a transport helicopter the size of a Cougar, a light battle tank, a mobile crane or two five-tonners with two 105mm field guns can be transported. There is also space for up to nine transport pallets or 120 troops with full equipment. For use in the ambulance-aircraft role the A400M can take 66 wounded on stretchers.

The main wheeled chassis can be lowered for loading purposes. It has on either side three individual dual chassis props with some tolerance for non-paved surfaces.

For the refuelling role tanks with a 12-tonne fuel capacity can be installed in the freight room. The tank probes can be installed below the wings in about two hours. Rate of fuel transfer is 1200 kgs/min.

As a swept-wing aircraft the A400M can cruise at Mach 0.72 and with a payload of 20 tonnes has a range of 6390 kms, with 30 tonnes the range is 4410 kms. The maximum range empty is given as 8820 kms. The A400M

can itself be refuelled in the air through a nozzle situated above the cockpit.

On 6 May 2003 Airbus Military decided to install the TP400-D6 10,000 shp (7500 kW) engine proposed by the European consortium Euro-Prop International (EPI). This is a completely new engine developed on the basis of proven technology in three-shaft design. Rolls-Royce, Snecma Moteurs, MTU Aero Engines and Industria de Turbopropulsores (ITP make up EPI. The three-shaft engine can be changed within twelve man hours. To reduce its heat signature, the hot jet of the engine is mixed with cold air to baffle heat-seeker rockets. 7500 hours were set aside for the testing programme with completion date 30 October 2007. This deadline could not be met. Many problems were encountered during the development and the first test flight of a C-130W fitted with the TP400-DC took place on 17 December 2008.

The A400M will have its own defensive system such as heat decoy rockets. The modular defence warning system DASS (Defensive Aids Sub-System) relays information from the radar, rocket and laser warning sensors into the cockpit where the appropriate counter-measures can be taken. Towed radar decoys can also be used. EADS Defence Electronics has provided the newly developed missile warning system MIRAS (Multi-Colour Infrared Alerting Sensor) based on the most up-to-date infrared technology. MIRAS has the modern superlattice-infrared detectors developed by AIM Infrared-Module GmbH. MIRAS is the first missile warning system worldwide to use Multi-Colour Infrared detection technology, and with the help of this novel combination a high level of detection probability, detection range and low rate of false alarms will be achieved. The missile warning system MIRAS will provide the European airlifter A400M with the most modern self-defence system in the world, decisively enhancing operational effectiveness and crew safety.

The last months before the programme began saw a continual falling away of orders. Originally it was expected to supply 288 aircraft to the partners in the cooperation. By mid-2001, after the cancellation of the Turkish contract, the procurement plan had fallen to 213 aircraft. When Italy and Portugal withdrew completely from the programme the total sales figure fell close to the break-even limit of 180, the minimum production figure for the commencement of the programme. This began on 27 May 2003, the procurement contract between Airbus Military and the mutual European procurement organisation OCCAR as representatives of the leading buyers being signed in Bonn on that day. At 10.15 a.m. on 11 December 2009 the first A400M, series number MSN1, made its successful maiden flight at Seville lasting three hours 47 minutes. The cockpit crew were Edward "Ed" Strongman, Chief Test Pilot of the Military Programme; Test Pilot Ignacio "Nacho" Lombo and Flight Trial Engineers Jean-Philippe Cottet, Eric Isorce, Didier Ronceray and Gérard Leskerpit.

By mid-2010 in addition to MSN 1 two other test aircraft – MSN 2 and MSN 3 – had been built, followed by MSN 4 at the end of 2010. A fifth machine will join the programme in 2011. About 3,700 test flight hours will be spent by this small fleet before the first machine is delivered to the French Air Force at the end of 2012. Then further military development flights will follow. The A400M will obtain certificates from both the civilian and military authorities.

LTG (Luft-Transport-Geschwader) 62 will be the first unit of the German Luftwaffe to be

Airbus Military A400M	
Purpose:	Airlifter and Refuelling Aircraft.
Crew:	Two pilots, one loading master and up to 120 troops.
Engine plant:	4 x Europrop International (EPI) TP400-D6, 11,000 shaft hp each (8200 kW).
Wingspan:	42.36 m; Length 42.2 m; Height 14.73 m; Wing area 221.5 sq.m.
Weight:	Empty 66.5 tonnes. Maximum take-off weight 130 tonnes. Useful payload, 37 tonnes.
Top speed:	826 kms/hr, (cruising) 780 kms/hr.
Range:	6390 kms with 20 tonne payload; 8820 kms without. Ceiling, 11,278 m.

equipped with the A400M. Whether this will really proceed all depends on how the testing goes. The next squadron in line is LTG 63, when LTG 61 will be disbanded.

Up to the time of writing, a total of 184 aircraft had been ordered by Belgium (7), Germany (60), France (50), Great Britain (25), Luxemburg (1), Malaysia (4), Spain (27) and Turkey (10). South Africa cancelled its order for eight aircraft.